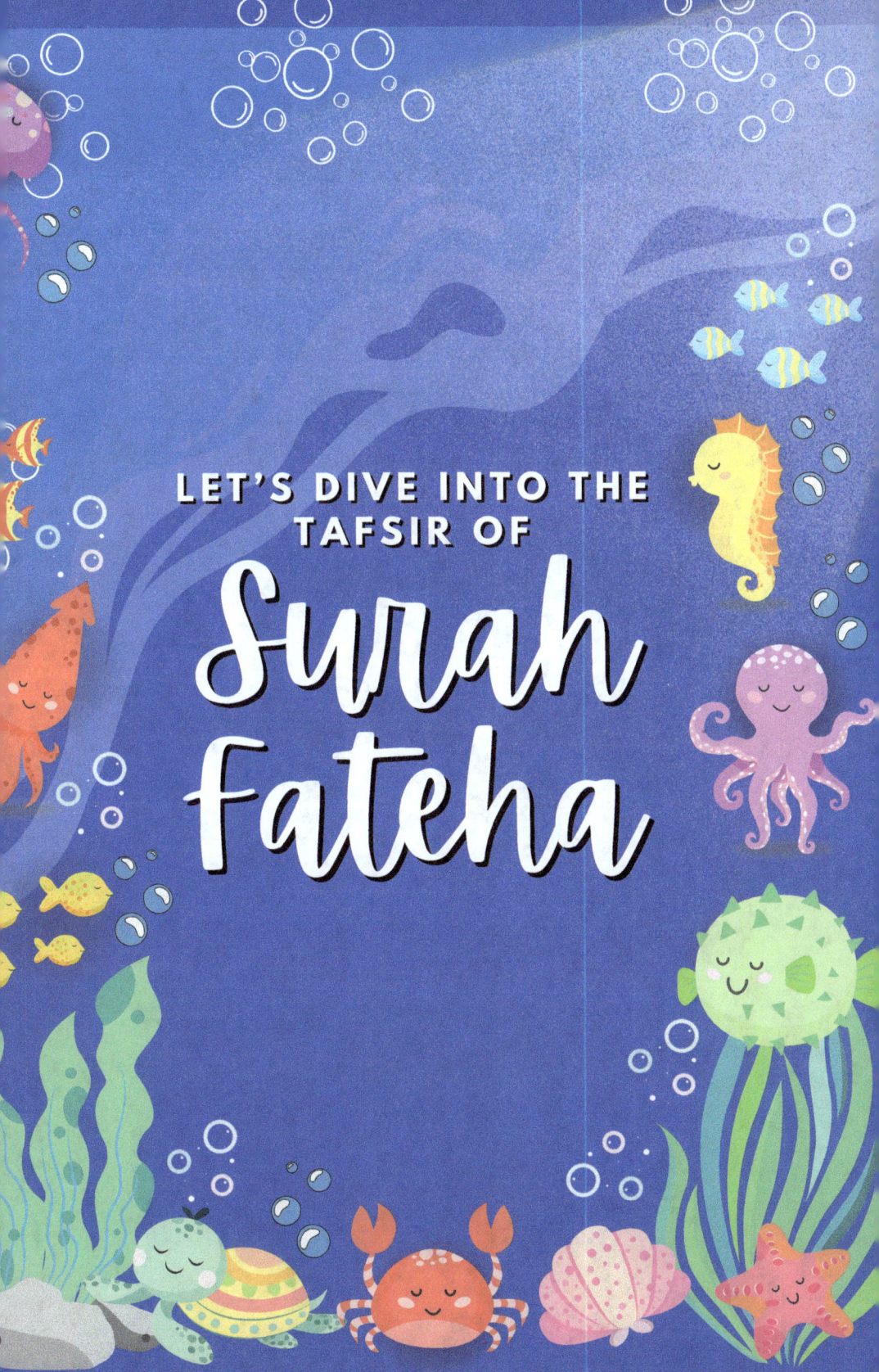

Take a moment and think. Allah could have chosen any ayah to begin the entire Holy Quran with, but He chose this beautiful ayah! How special must this ayah be! And the same way, our parents and teachers always tell us to begin our work with the name of Allah, by saying Bismillah! But why is that? Why should we start our work by saying Bismillah? Let's try and find out!

WHY SHOULD WE BEGIN OUR WORK WITH BISMILLAH?

1

When we say Bismillah, we are calling upon Allah for help! And that too, using His beautiful names Ar Rahman and Ar Raheem! We are asking the Most Merciful to help us with our work. And so, Allah will help us make our work easier for us, whether we are doing our homework, an exam, or helping someone! In fact, if we are are eating, he will make our food be filled with blessings too!

2

It makes us realise that we need Allah's help for everything! If He doesn't help us, we won't be able to eat, walk, sleep, or do anything! He is the One who has all control! And so, we will also remember to thank Him after completing our work!

3

When we give someone a gift, we write their name on it. The same way, if we take Allah's name before every act of ours, they will be sincerely for Allah! Our niyyah will be to please Allah, and then even something like brushing our teeth will become a beautiful deed for Allah!

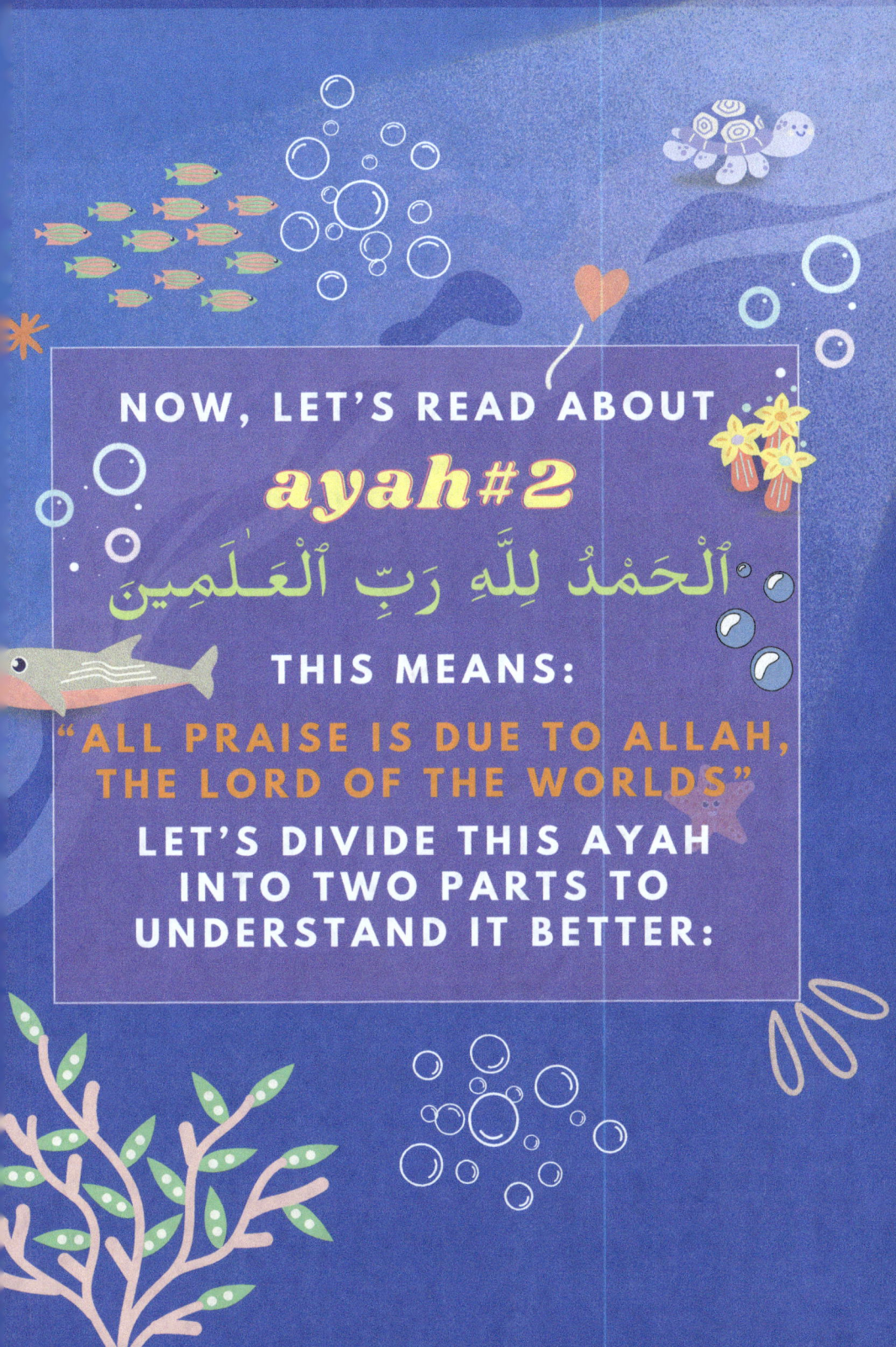

We recite the phrase Alhamdulillah somewhere else too! Can you recall? Yes! While reciting the Tasbih of Bibi Fatima Zahra (sa) after every Namaz! Now we know, it means, all praise is for Allah! But why?

Let's think about it. Allah made such deep oceans with so many different creaturs that we don't even know of! There's a whole universe! Such high mountains, such deep oceans, skies that are in the sky without anything holding them up! Aren't those such amazing creations of Allah? They are! And therefore, we say, all praises are due to Allah!

The Lord of the Worlds. We see that Allah did not just create everyone and everything, but He takes care of each and everyone, the tiniest insect and the largest animals! He makes sure every creature gets their food, He makes sure we all get oxygen to breathe, He makes sure we are taken care of! He nurtures us so carefully! That is what it means when we say Allah is our Rabb. He is our Nurturing Lord. So, when we say this Ayah, we should say it with all our heart, thanking Him for taking care of us so well! He never leaves us alone.

Ar-Rahman and Ar-Raheem both come from the word "Rahm", which means mercy! So in this Ayah, Allah refers to His mercy. He is so merciful, that He has gifted us with so many things! For example, He gave us the Holy Quran, our beloved RasulAllah (saww), and the Ahlul Bayt (as) to guide us! He gave us food to eat when we are hungry, water to drink when we are thirsty! He is so merciful that He fulfills all our needs! Infact not just needs, He also gifts us with things that we want! So, when we recite this Ayah, we should remember Allah's mercy towards us.

But you might be thinking, "What's the difference between Ar-Rahman and Ar-Raheem?" That's a brilliant question!

Let's see. Allah has two kinds of mercy. One, is His general mercy to everyone, for example he makes sure everyone gets oxygen! That is His mercy for everyone, and an example of Allah being Ar Rahman! The second kind of mercy is the special mercy that Allah gives only to His believers! For example, Allah helped the Muslims win the Battle of Badr! That is an example of Allah being Ar Raheem! Now you know the difference between Ar Rahman and Ar Raheem!

"Maalik" means the Master or the Owner! Allah can do anything He wants because He owns all of us! "Youm id Deen" refers to the Day of Judgement! He not only owns us, but He owns everyone and everything, including The Day of Judgement! He can do anything He wishes! He can save whoever He wants!

So, let's look at the Surah up till now. First, we began in the name of Allah. Then, we praised Him and remembered how much He takes care of us! Next we called upon Allah with His beautiful names of mercy, Ar Rahman and Ar Raheem! And now, we are calling upon Him as the Master of the Day of Judgement!

Let's compare this to how we would ask our mother for something we really want! First, we call her to bring her attention to us, so she listens to us! Then, we thank her for how much work she does for us, so that she comes in a good mood and let's us have what we want! Then we say, "Mama you are so nice, you are so kind!" to remind her of her mercy! And then, we remind her of her power and authority! "Mama, you have the power to allow me!" Do you see a similarity? This is exactly what is done in Surah Fateha! But what are we asking Allah for? We are asking Allah for safety from the Fire of Hell! We are asking for security on the Day of Judgement!

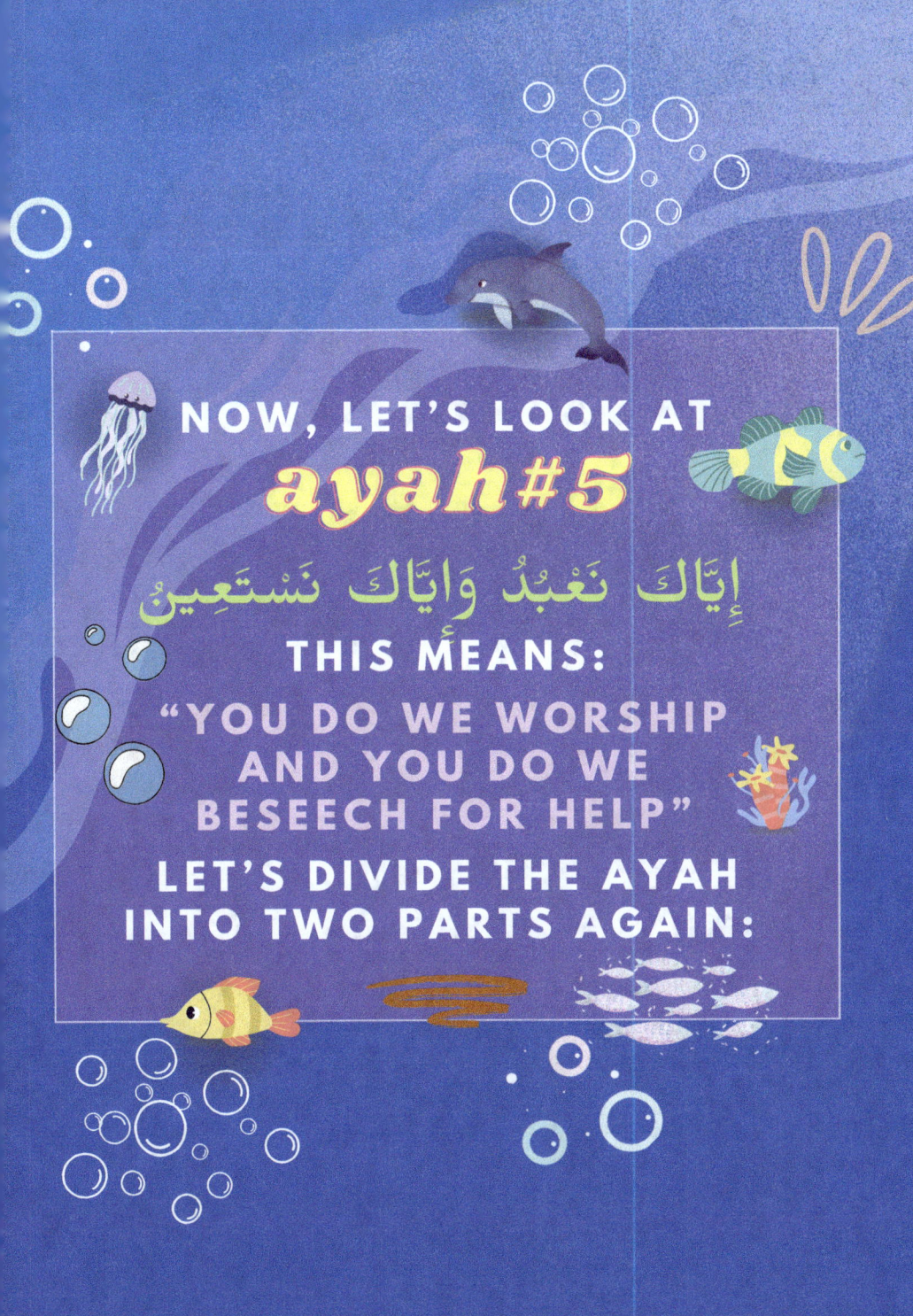

This ayah can also remind us of how we continue to ask our mother! We make sure that she says yes to us, and we don't leave until she says yes! The same way, we continue to beg Allah so that we make sure that He says yes and grants us what we are asking Him for!

With this ayah, we are continuing to beg Allah! We say, Oh Allah, we don't have anybody except for You! We put all our hopes in You! We are begging You, beseeching You for help! But still, we have not clearly mentioned what we are asking Allah for? Why is that?

First, we praised Allah so much, called Him by His beautiful names of mercy, and told him that He is our only hope, so that we make sure that He will not say no to us! Now that that part is done, let's see in the next ayah, what we are asking Allah for! It is definitely something so important that we first made sure that Allah says yes! Are we asking Allah for a chocolate, or our favourite clothes? Let's see!

We finally come to ask Allah for this extremely important blessing, and that is the Straight Path! This ayah teaches us that it is so important to pray to Allah to keep us on the Straight Path, but not jusy pray to Him, but to also try our best to be on the Straight Path!

This ayah sets a clear target for us! A clear goal! Now we know, if there is something that we should aim to achieve in this life, it is the Straight Path! All our efforts should be directed towards this goal! But what is the Straight Path? Can you make a guess? The Ahlul Bayt (as) gives us the answer to this question! They say, "We are the Straight Path!"

And so, following the straight path means following the Ahlul Bayt (as). That means that all our efforts should be to become like them! First, we should learn about them, about how they were, and then, before doing anything we should think, would my Imam (as) have done this in this situation? If yes, then only I would do it, and if not, then not at all! For example, if I am angry, I will remember the story of Rasulallah (saww) when he controlled his anger and remained patient, and then would also calm myself down. This is how we can stay on the Straight Path!

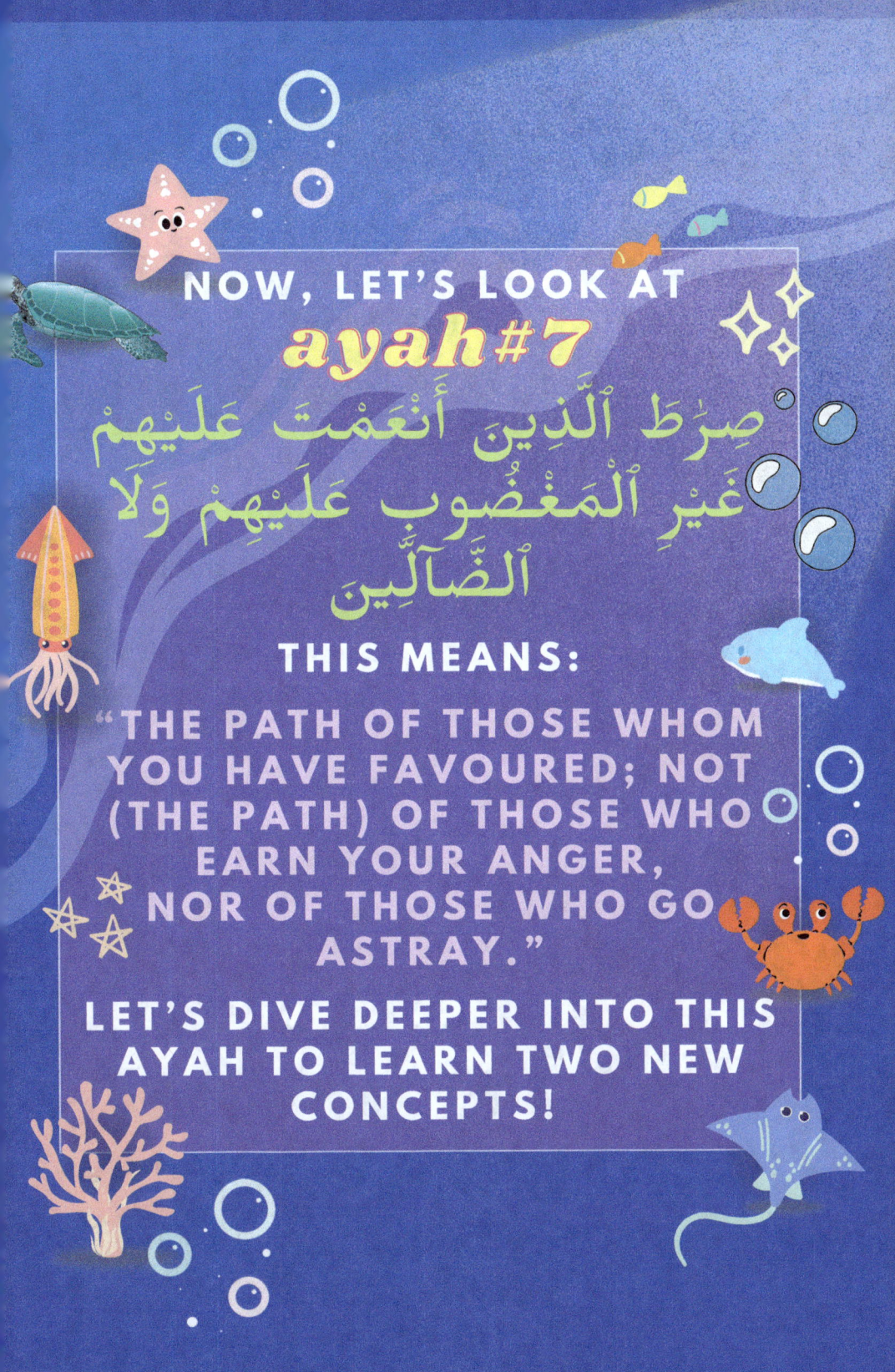

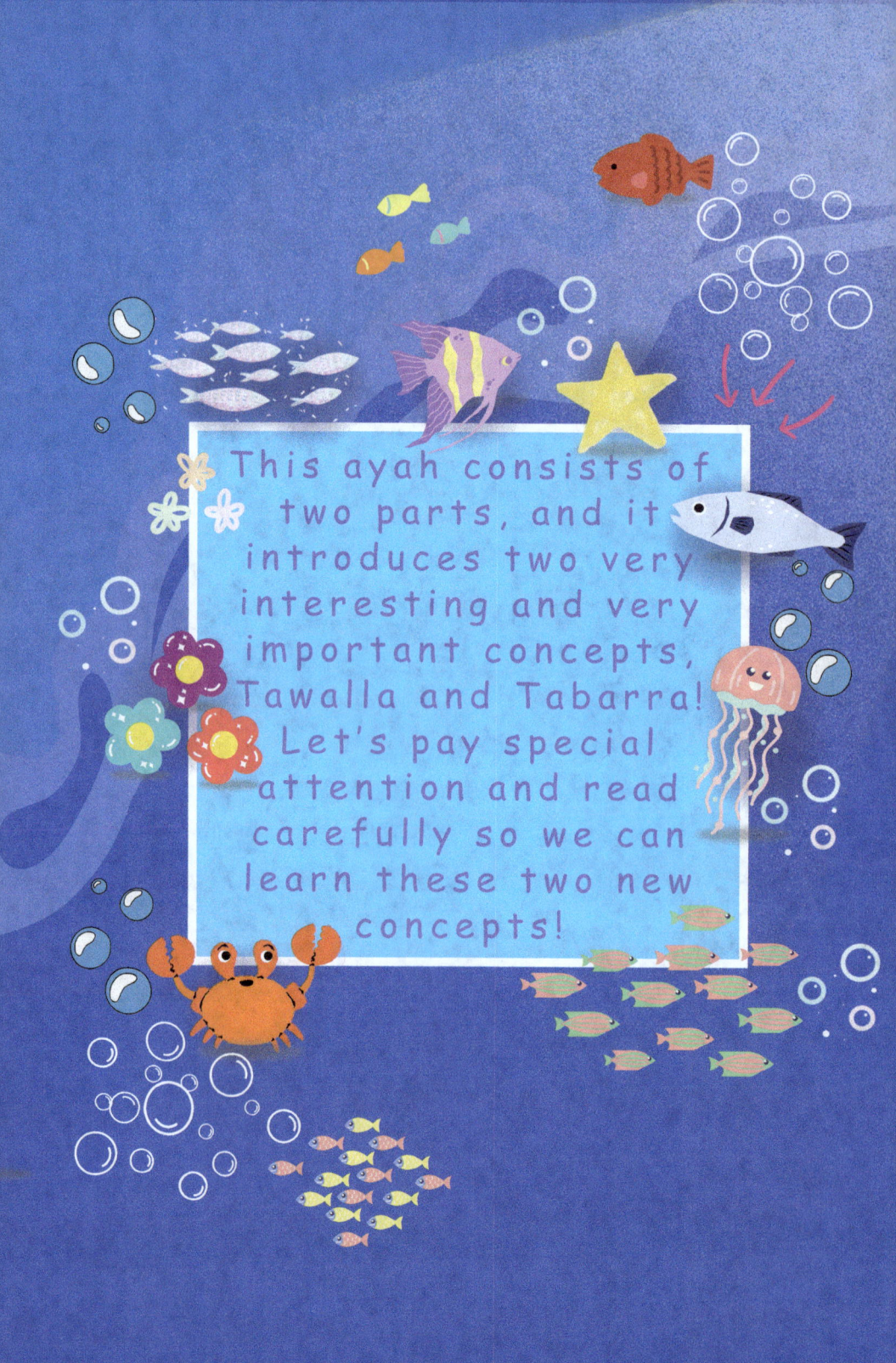

This ayah consists of two parts, and it introduces two very interesting and very important concepts, Tawalla and Tabarra! Let's pay special attention and read carefully so we can learn these two new concepts!

It's time to go in a level deeper, so let's get ready! If we pay attention, this ayah has two parts: "The path of those upon whom You have bestowed Your favours" and "Not of those inflicted by Your wrath, nor of those gone astray."

First of all, who are those upon whom Allah has bestowed His special favours? They are the Ahlul Bayt (as)! Allah also says that in other places in the Holy Quran, such as in Ayah e Tatheer (33:33). That confirms that the Straight Path is the Path of the Ahlul Bayt (as)! That clarifies the first part of the ayah.

What about the second part of the ayah? Who are the people who went astray and Allah punished them? They are all those people who opposed the Ahlul Bayt (as) and fought against them! This explains the second part of the ayah! Now, the important concepts that we learn in this ayah are Tawalla and Tabarra! The first part of the ayah teaches us Tawalla, which means to love the Ahlul Bayt (as)! And the second part of the ayah teaches us Tabarra, which means to oppose the enemies of the Ahlul Bayt (as)! The Quran teaches us these two concepts in such a simple and beautiful manner!

LET'S SEE WHAT OUR BELOVED RASULALLAH (SAWW) HAS SAID ABOUT SURAH FATEHA:

> Imam Ali ar-Rida (a.s.) narrates through his forefathers from Amir al-Mu'minin Ali (a.s.) that he said: "I heard the Prophet of Allah saying: "Allah, Mighty and Great, has said: "I have divided the Opening of the Book (Surah Fateha) between Myself and My servant; so, its half is for Me and the (other) half is for My servant. And My servant shall get what he asks for."

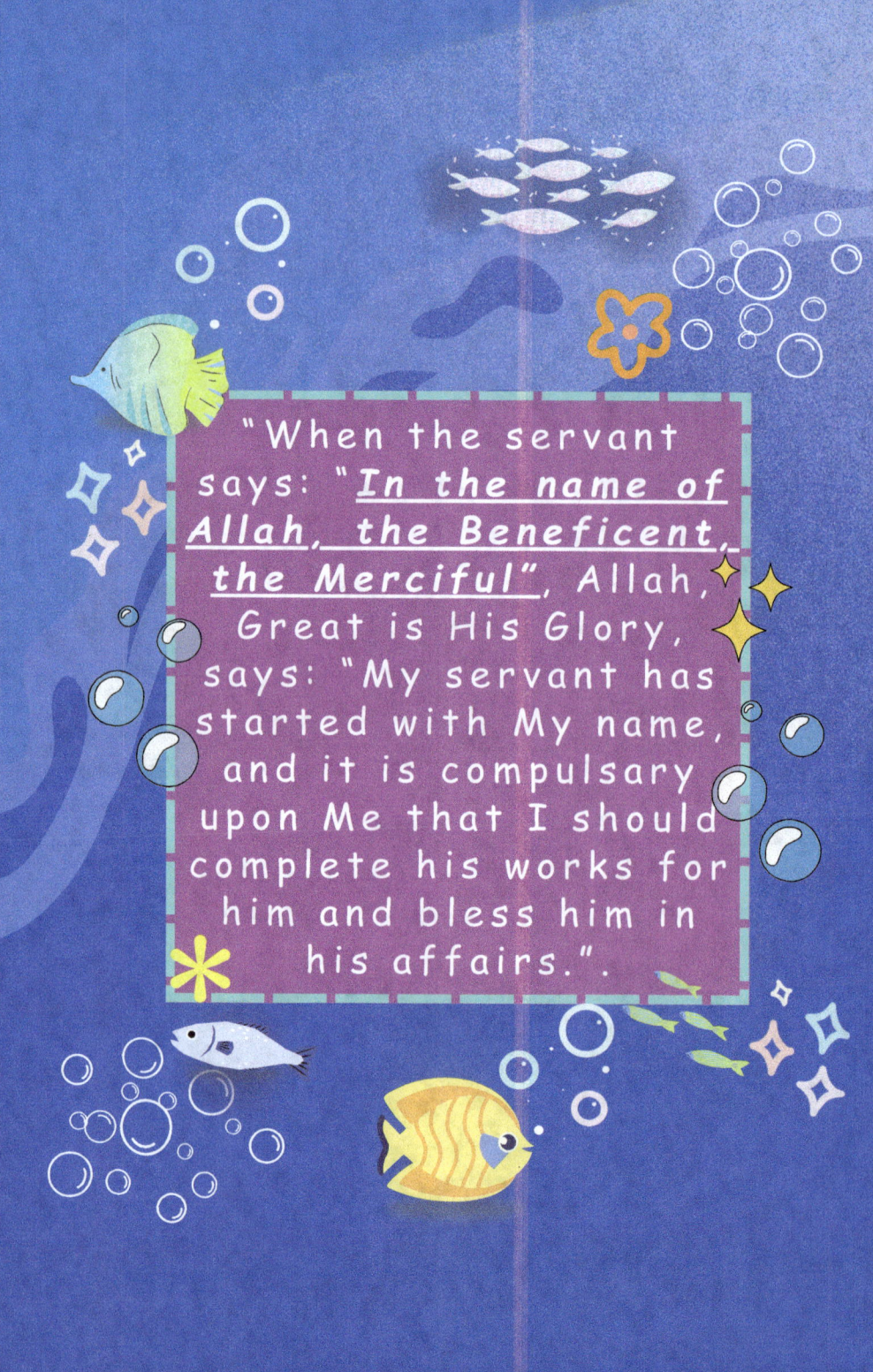

"When the servant says: "<u>In the name of Allah, the Beneficent, the Merciful</u>", Allah, Great is His Glory, says: "My servant has started with My name, and it is compulsary upon Me that I should complete his works for him and bless him in his affairs."

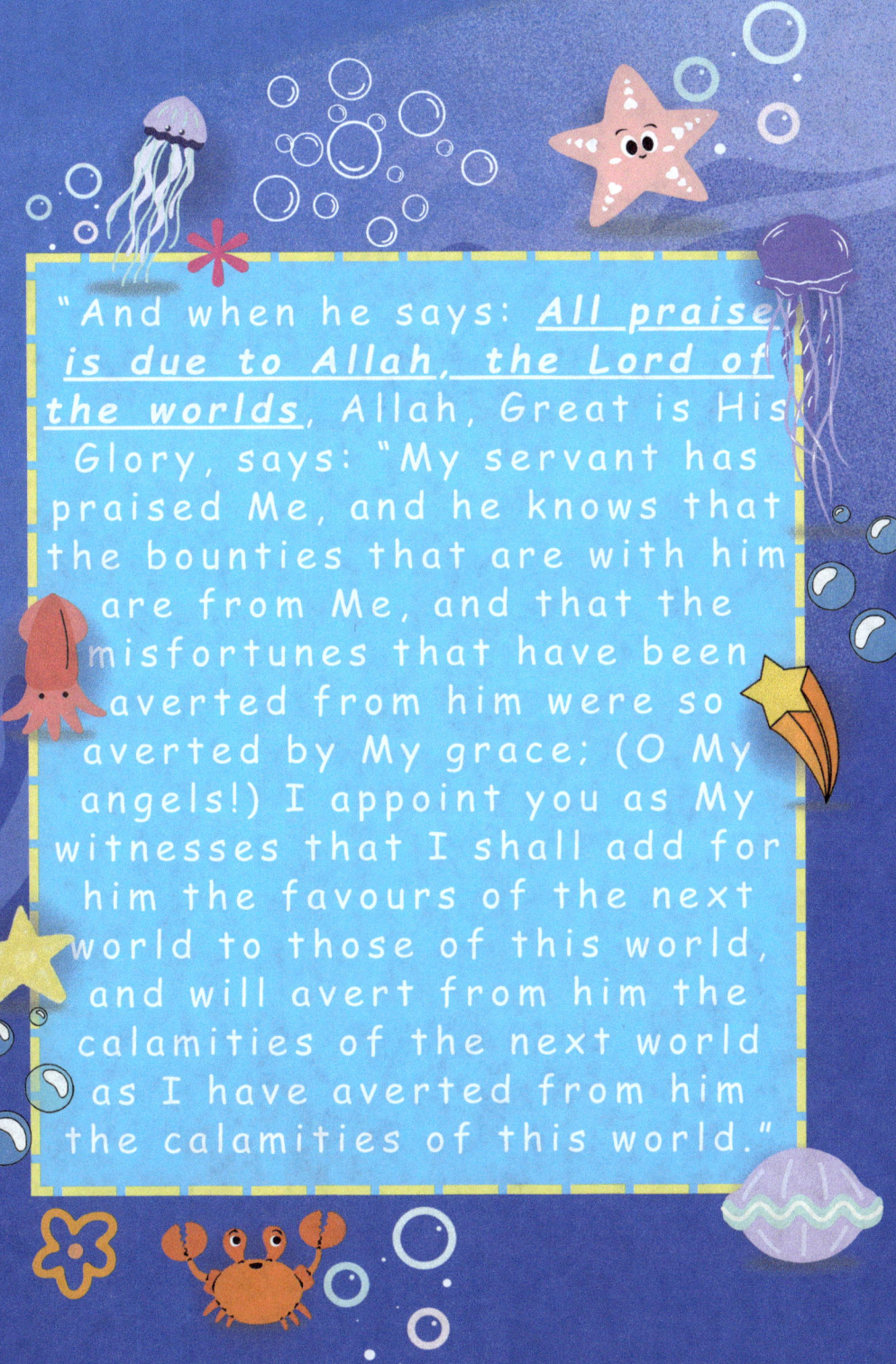

"And when he says: <u>**All praise is due to Allah, the Lord of the worlds**</u>, Allah, Great is His Glory, says: "My servant has praised Me, and he knows that the bounties that are with him are from Me, and that the misfortunes that have been averted from him were so averted by My grace; (O My angels!) I appoint you as My witnesses that I shall add for him the favours of the next world to those of this world, and will avert from him the calamities of the next world as I have averted from him the calamities of this world."

"And when he says, <u>**The Beneficent, the Merciful**</u>, Allah, Great is His Glory, s: "My servant bore witness for Me that I am the Beneficent, the Merciful; I make you My witness that I will most surely augment his share in My mercy, and I will most certainly increase his portion in My bounties."

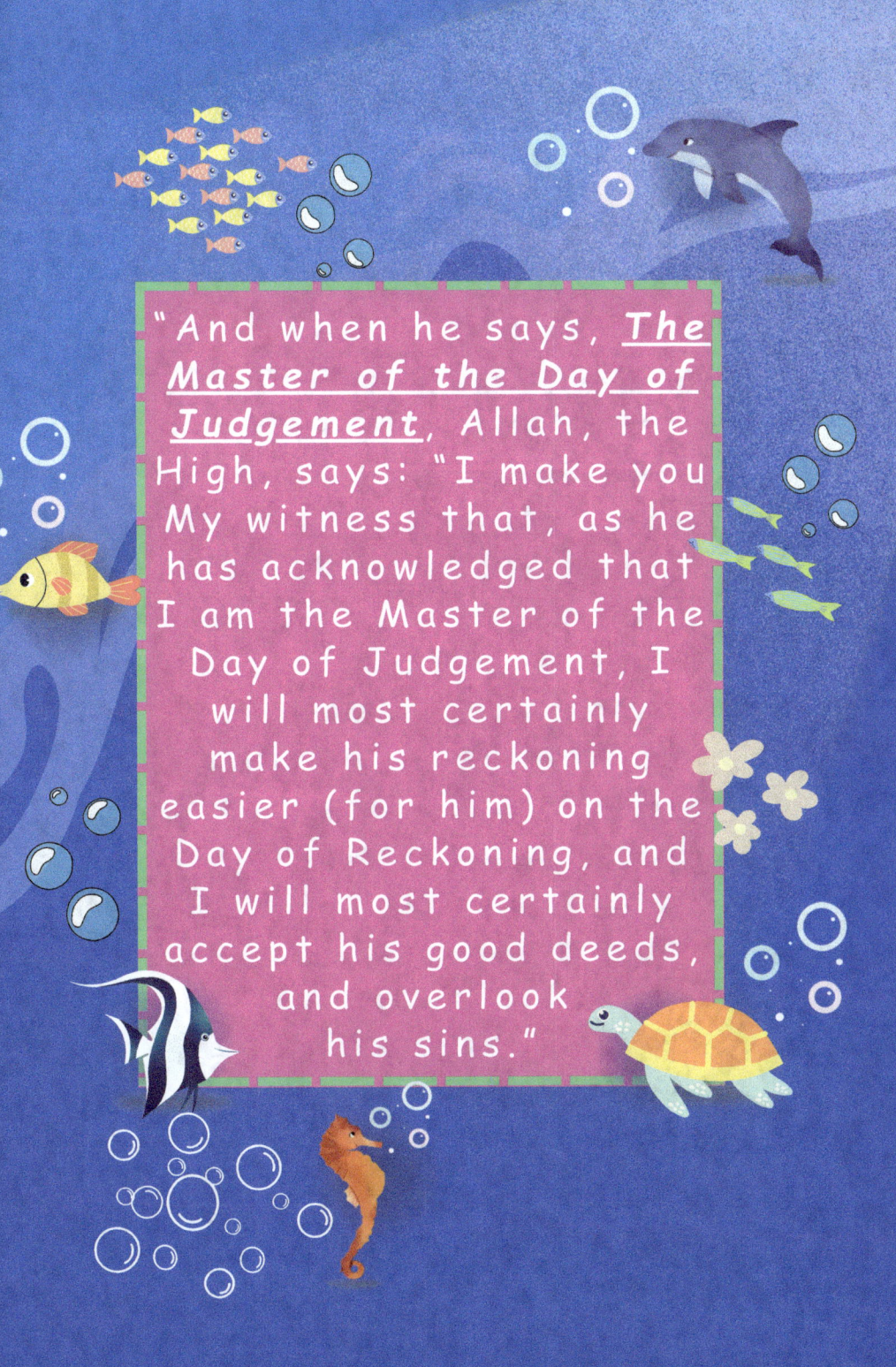

"And when he says, <u>**The Master of the Day of Judgement**</u>, Allah, the High, says: "I make you My witness that, as he has acknowledged that I am the Master of the Day of Judgement, I will most certainly make his reckoning easier (for him) on the Day of Reckoning, and I will most certainly accept his good deeds, and overlook his sins."

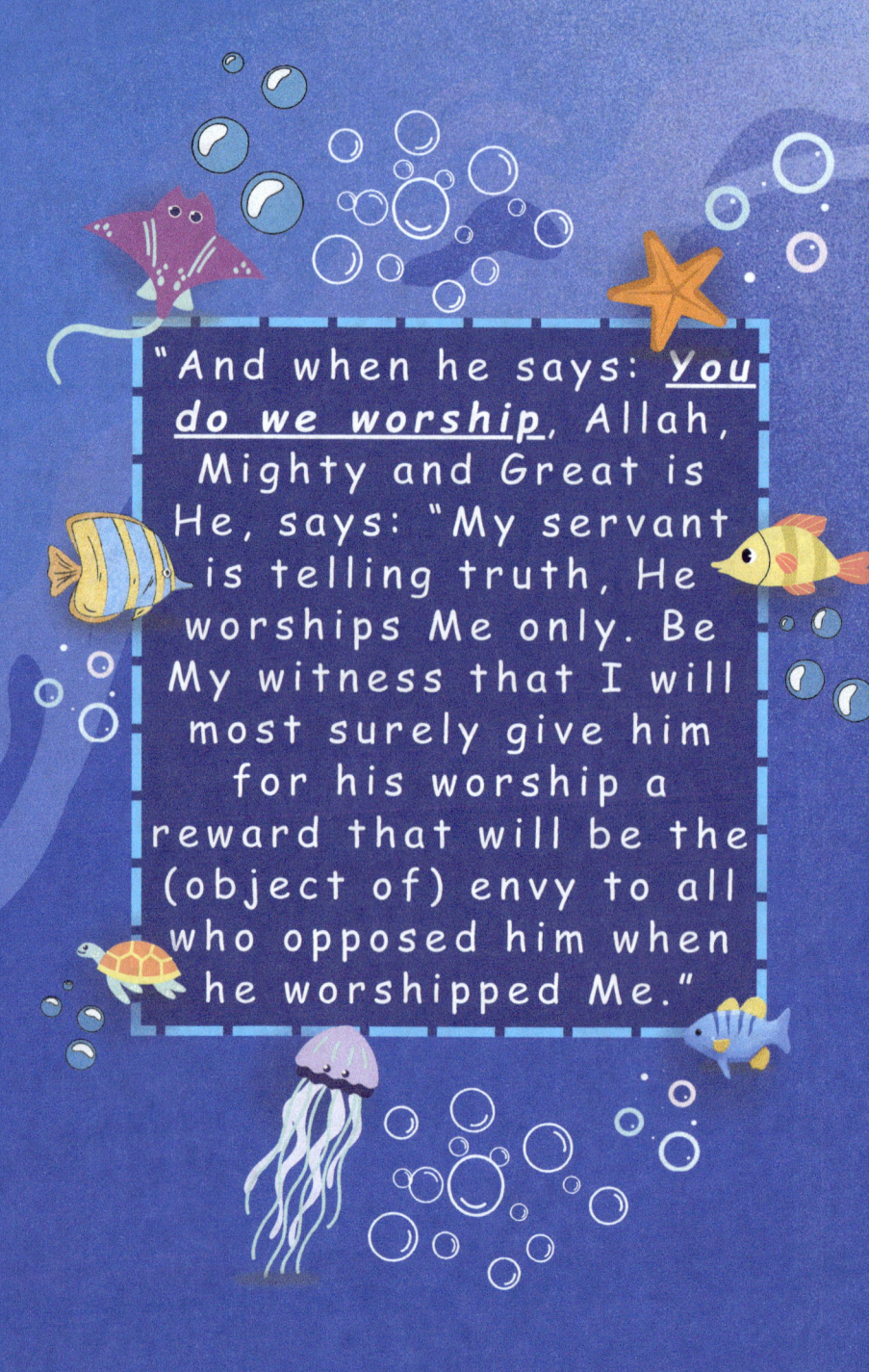

"And when he says: <u>you do we worship</u>, Allah, Mighty and Great is He, says: "My servant is telling truth, He worships Me only. Be My witness that I will most surely give him for his worship a reward that will be the (object of) envy to all who opposed him when he worshipped Me."

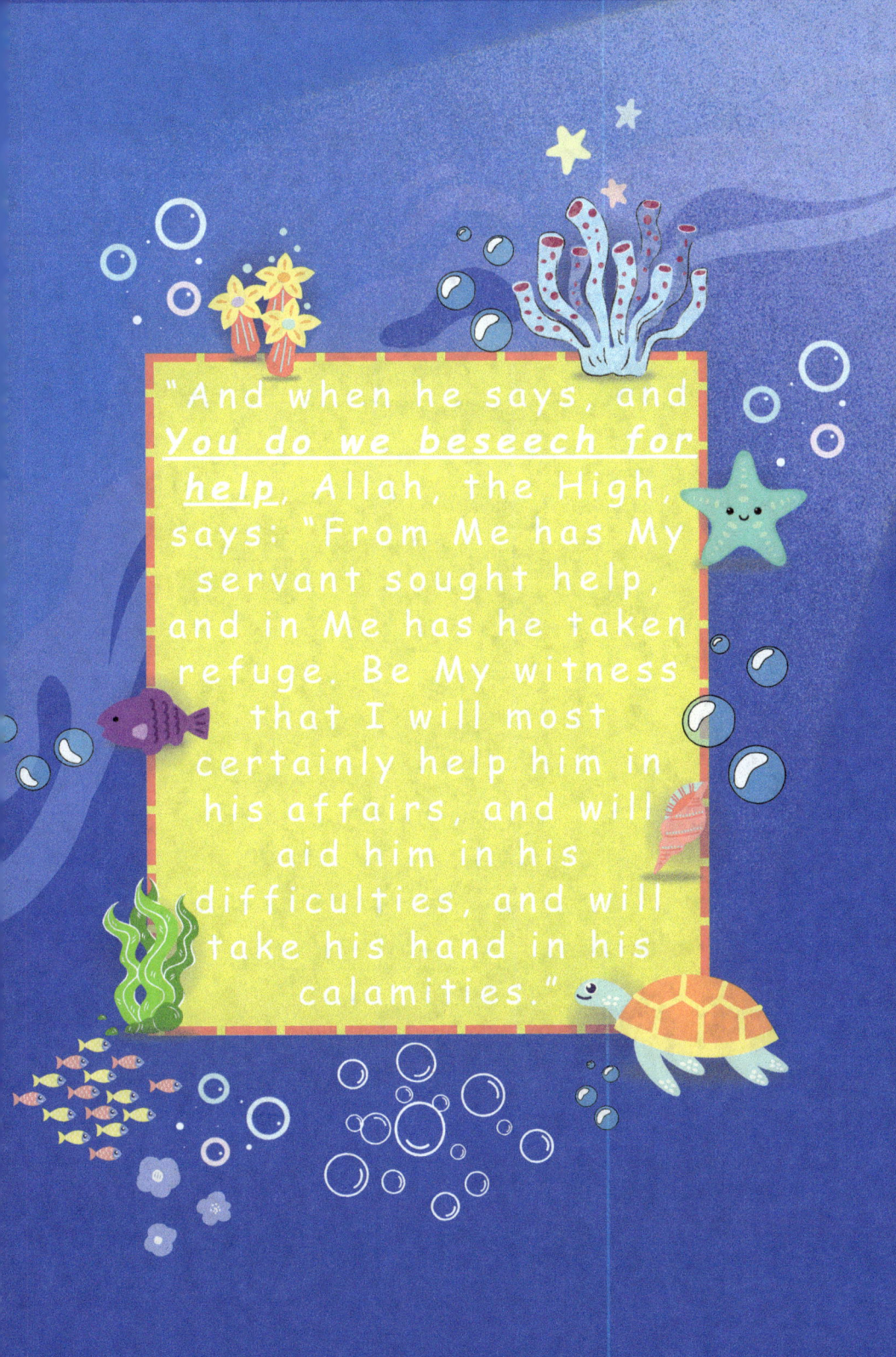

"And when he says, and **You do we beseech for help**, Allah, the High, says: "From Me has My servant sought help, and in Me has he taken refuge. Be My witness that I will most certainly help him in his affairs, and will aid him in his difficulties, and will take his hand in his calamities."

"And when he says, <u>Guide us to the right path, the path of those upon whom Thou hast bestowed favours, not of those inflicted by your wrath, nor of those gone astray.</u> Allah, Mighty and Great is He, says: "This (part) is for My servant, and My servant shall have what he asks for; and I have answered (the prayer of) My servant, and have given him what he hopes for and have protected him from what he is afraid of."

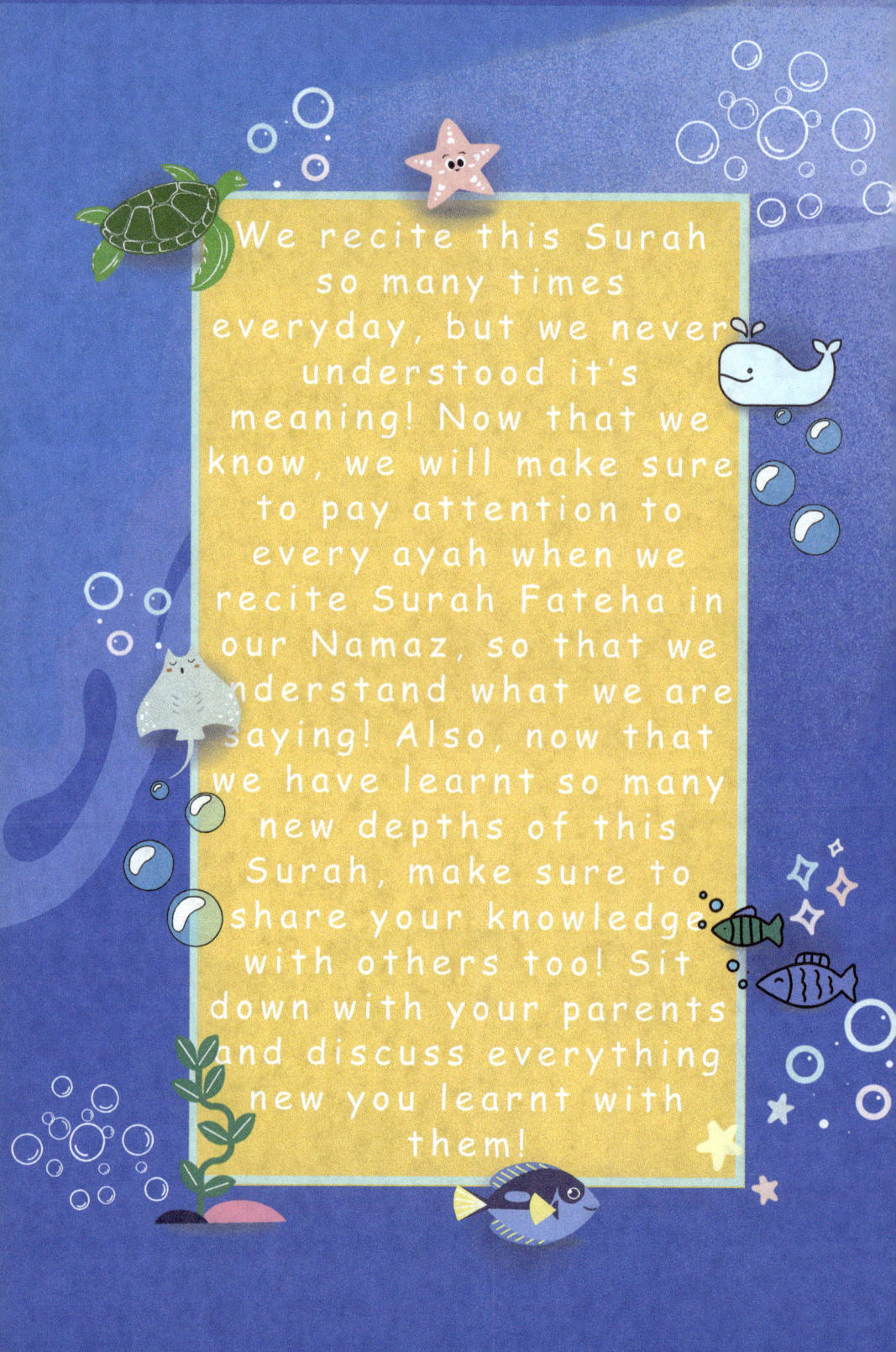

We recite this Surah so many times everyday, but we never understood it's meaning! Now that we know, we will make sure to pay attention to every ayah when we recite Surah Fateha in our Namaz, so that we understand what we are saying! Also, now that we have learnt so many new depths of this Surah, make sure to share your knowledge with others too! Sit down with your parents and discuss everything new you learnt with them!

www.ingramcontent.com/pod-product-compliance
Lightning Source LLC
Chambersburg PA
CBHW072003060526
44107CB00150B/387